Kika

My First Word Book

by

Fukiko Yamamoto

chronicle books · san francisco

Kika's World

Kika's Family
Kika
baby
mother
father
kiss
hug
friends
share

Kika's House
window
door
table
chair
telephone
television
key
clock
lamp
bed
blocks

book
toys
doll
teddy bear
mirror
toilet
sink
bathtub
soap
toothbrush
hairbrush

Kika Gets Dressed
pajamas
shirt
shorts
hat
coat
boots
socks
shoes

Kika Eats
eat
drink
egg
banana
orange
apple
ice cream
cereal
cup
plate
bowl
spoon

Kika Goes Outside
moon
sun
stars
cloud
rain
snow

cold
hot
wind
flower
tree
leaf
house
mailbox
dirty
clean
cat
dog
bird
dragonfly
balloon
ball

Kika Gets Around

stroller
bicycle
car

bus
train
airplane

Kika Takes Action

sit
stand
run
walk
draw
paint
empty
fill
jump
climb
bounce
swim
push
pull
dance
sing

talk
listen
smile
frown
laugh
cry

Kika Feels

happy
sad
silly
mad
excited
sleepy

Kika Says

hello
good-bye

Kika

baby

friends

table

key

bed

book

teddy bear

mirror

bathtub

toothbrush

pajamas

shirt

shorts

hat

coat

boots

socks

shoes

eat

drink

egg

banana

orange

apple

ice cream

cereal

cup

plate

bowl

spoon

moon

sun

stars

cloud

rain

snow

cold

hot

wind

flower

tree

leaf

house

mailbox

dirty

clean

cat

dog

bird

dragonfly

balloon

ball

stroller

bicycle

car

bus

train

airplane

sit

stand

run

walk

draw

paint

empty

fill

jump

climb

bounce

swim

push

pull

dance

sing

talk

listen

smile

frown

laugh

cry

happy

sad

silly

mad

excited

sleepy

hello

good-bye

Dedicated to Delphina Kika Mimosa

The Kika character and all illustrations copyright © 2006 by
Fukiko Yamamoto and Pocko.
All rights reserved.

Creative direction by Nicola Schwartz.
Book design by Olga Norman.
Pocko People, www.pocko.com

Manufactured in China.
ISBN-10 0-8118-5298-9
ISBN-13 978-0-8118-5298-2

Library of Congress Cataloging-in-Publication Data available.

Distributed in Canada by Raincoast Books
9050 Shaughnessy Street, Vancouver, British Columbia V6P 6E5

10 9 8 7 6 5 4 3 2 1

Chronicle Books LLC
85 Second Street, San Francisco, California 94105

www.chroniclekids.com

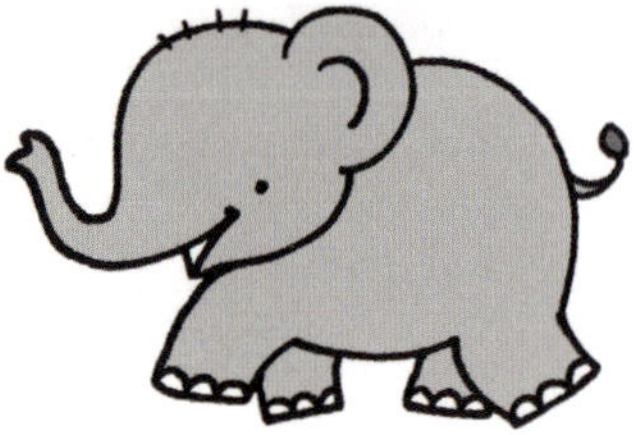
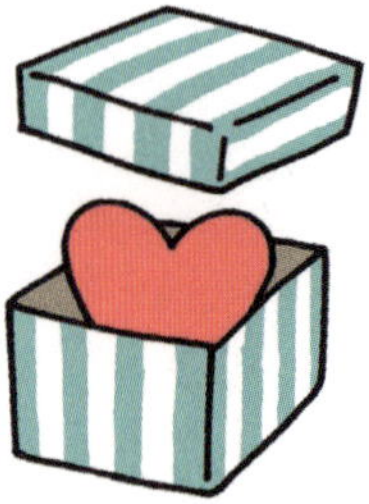

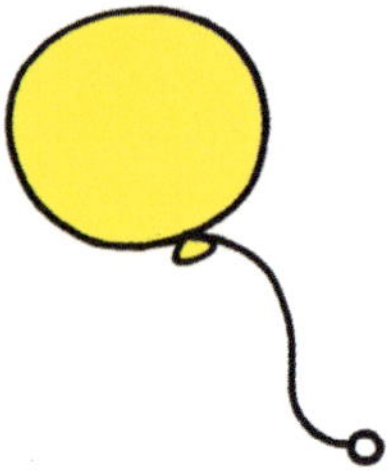
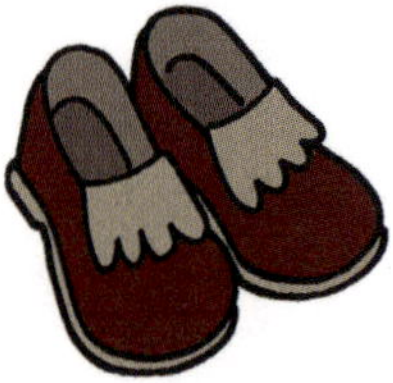
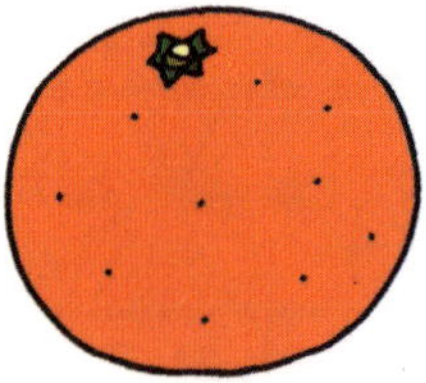
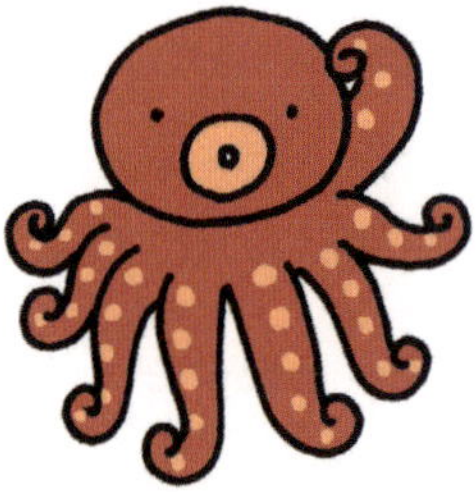
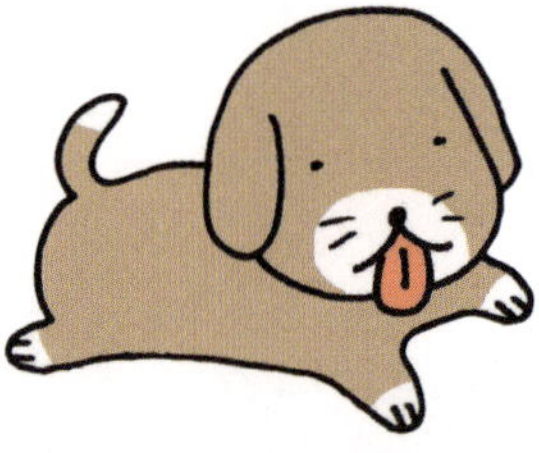
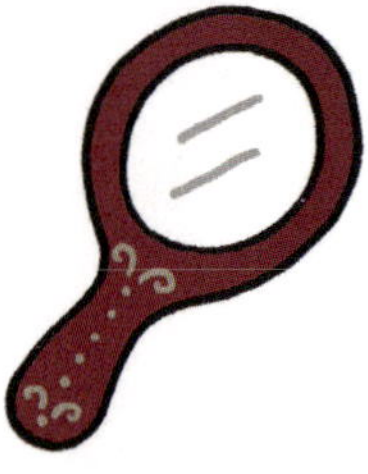
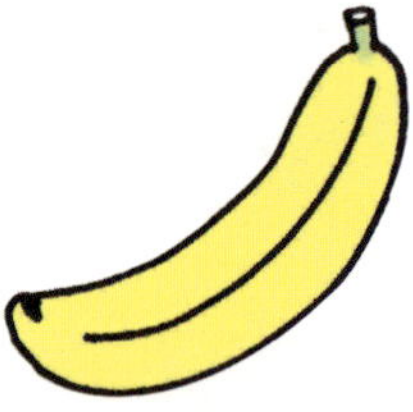